T0114847

Poetry, one of the most important and time-honored forms of literature in the world – has brought us many greats like Dr. Maya Angelou, Langston Hughes and Toni Morrison, to name a few. Add Alexander Sullivan to that list. Why? Because Mr. Sullivan is one of the most masterful poets in the 21st Century whose work is strong, relatable and compelling examples of life that connects everyone.

I got chills reading each one of his pieces that significantly relates to every aspect of my life and/or those I know. From the first poem titled "Thoughts of a Young Black Man" to "Friendship" to the last one called "Words," I was glued to the book from start to finish.

Every line of poetry written by Mr. Sullivan tells a vivid story, exploring many different aspects of his life about love and heartache, family, friendships and so much more. This book is epic and would make a beautiful gift to those seeking or providing inspiration. It is a must-read!

**- LaToya E. Sizer PhD EL**

# THOUGHTS OF A YOUNG BLACK MAN

ALEXANDER E. SULLIVAN

author HOUSE

AuthorHouse™
1663 Liberty Drive
Bloomington, IN 47403
www.authorhouse.com
Phone: 833-262-8899

Published by AuthorHouse  04/22/2021

ISBN: 978-1-6655-1590-0 (sc)
ISBN: 978-1-6655-1591-7 (e)

# DEDICATION

This book of poetry is dedicated to my younger self. A young man seeking to discover his purpose in life as he struggled in his journey to manhood. A lost soul who was in a small boat in the middle of an ocean and seemingly no one was searching for him. However, the hand of God was upon him and brought him safely to shore. His hand remains eternally.

"You go before me and follow me. You place your hand of blessing on my head. Such knowledge is too wonderful for me to understand! You saw me before I was born. Every day of my life was recorded in your book. Every moment was laid out before a single day had passed." Psalm 139:5-6, 16 (NLT)

# AM I

Am I young, am I old?
Am I different or from a mold?
I search heaven from the depths of my soul,
Am I young, am I old?

Am I blind to what I see?
Is this happiness or disguised misery?
Am I coming or am I going,
Am I foolish for not knowing?

Should I laugh, stop from crying,
Tell the truth or hide by lying?
Life has contrasts, always twofold,
Am I young or am I old?

# BEING FREE

Being free means doing anything you want to,
Yet realizing there is a limit to what you can do.
It means being able to say what you like,
Yet not anything to hurt someone.
Being able to go anywhere you care to,
But never trespassing on another's ground.
It gives you the opportunity to fulfill your dreams
without losing sight of reality.
Being able to say, "I will, I can, I must."
Being free means being sad for those who are not.

# BLACK AND PROUD

Some Negroes are ashamed of their color "Black."
For them, it means a link to slavery, inferiority and hardships.
Well, I'm proud to be Black for it's my link to pride and perseverance.
Being Black is a God-given gift,
Which no one can take away from me.
Being Black is my link to wonderful cultures in Africa,
Our overcoming of hardships in America.
It's my link to a proud people who were once slaves and
who now again are becoming a proud people.
Being Black means that no matter how
difficult life may get, I can overcome.

# BREAKING UP

Are you leaving me today?
What can I say to keep you by my side?
Surely, you know it is you I need in my life.
If leaving me satisfies your needs, then go,
It is you I want to please.
I tried to give you the best a man could offer,
Soon you will realize life on earth isn't heaven.
It is sad to break up after so long of loving each other,
In this game we call life, I'm sure I'll find another.
Let us part the way we met,
Lots of understanding and mutual respect.

# BUFFALO SOLDIERS

They did not ride on large white horses
Nor did they carry big shiny swords,
They went quietly about doing their jobs while
singing praises to the Lord.
Their eyes were tired, fighting for the freedom
and liberty of their country…rights
that they could not enjoy.
These men were not ordinary troopers nor did they care to be.
These men were Buffalo Soldiers serving in the U.S. Calvary.
Side by side they fought and died with their fellow counterparts.
They received medals of the highest honors;
Many received Purple Hearts.
They had to wage a twofold war, one they didn't win,
Their declared enemy was to the front, natural enemy from ranks within.
Pressured by racism, rejection, and enemy rounds,
All this they took in stride.
These men were Buffalo Soldiers, fighting for their country with pride.

# CAN YOU SLOW DANCE

Will you hold me when life's trials are raging about?
Would you whisper words of encouragement in my lonely night?
Can you find the time to share your secret thoughts?
Together can we slow dance as we journey along this walk

You entered my life not a moment too soon,
Brought joy and sometimes pain which helped me grow.
I find you thoughtful in the most sensuous ways,
Together, we can slow dance throughout the lasting days.

Just knowing you has made me a better man,
For you have challenged my heart as no one can.
The affectionate sound of your voice rings notes of romance,
I wonder can we together slow dance.

Time nor space won't allow me to enumerate,
For I long to snuggle in the warmth of your embrace.
Your eloquent demeanor mesmerize my imagination dare I say,
Can we together love one another as we slow dance the night away?

—

# COMPUTER TIME

I have a personal computer,

Not just one but two.

Yet my life has become too impersonal with so many things to do,

There's Facebook, Twitter, and Myspace with all "my friends"

However during moment of sadness there's

no one on whom I can depend.

Ah yes, the computer is a convenient and accessible tool,

One can get a formal education without

having stepped foot in a school.

People display their lives for the entire world to see,

The shallowness of their content is quite evident.

Online dating is a high tech version of what pen-pal used to be,

Unfortunately the ability to convey thoughts

with pen and paper has become history.

For all the good it does, there exist a dark side.

Evil masks itself in the convenience computers provide.

Families communicate more but talk less,

The virtual world has become their refuge in a time of emptiness.

Predators prey online seeking whom they can devour,

Yet the computer provides a level playing field

for the innovative entrepreneur.

The computer, like the TV, has opened up a brave New world,

Prayerfully people will use it as a tool not as their all in all.

# FEAR NOT

Fear not man for life nor death he can give,
Fear not the obstacles of life for they provide challenges to conquer.
Fear not being alone for then you can think and dream,
Fear not heights if you are to attain success.
Fear not failure if you are to climb the heights,
Fear not death for it cannot hold you.
Fear only God removing His love from you for without it
You are doomed to destruction.

# FRIEND

Lift up your cast down eyes,
You are not alone in your thoughts.
I understand your disappointments,
For I too suffered along this walk.

Do not fear life's challenges,
Take a firm hold of its yoke.
It is the strength one possesses
Allows you to overcome and grow.

Your quiet spirit and timid soul,
Add to these a determined heart.
Dare to dream, realize your goals,
Today is the day to start.

If need be, I will be here,
Offering encouragement along the way.
Put your hand in God's hand,
For tomorrow is a brighter day.

# FRIENDSHIP

"There's a kind of quiet sadness in a sunset, yet warmth."
The kind of warmth true friends feels when they are together.
That is the way it should be between friends,
someone who will stand by you no matter.
We have heard it said, "A friend in need is a friend indeed,"
We all need a special someone to identify with.
Let us not be deceived by a person, who becomes
your friend only in time of sorrow,
That friendship is like earth's surrounding elements;
Sunshine today, a cold spell tomorrow.
Friendship is a must in a troublesome world as we have today,
We should try to become someone's companion in a peaceful way.
It does not take much, just a warm friendly smile,
Friendship is an investment we all need in our lives.
It helps to heed to the saying that holds true,
"It is best to love others as you would have them love you."

# GRANDMA

Hard work, no play,
Grandma did not cut any slack,
Made our living with our backs.
Cutting grass, chopping wood,
Sun beating on our hides,
It did not matter to her,
Work kept our needs supplied.
Went to church every Sunday,
Unless sick and about to die,
Fire and brimstone thrown my way,
All because I told a lie.
Our friends smoked and they would cuss,
This she did not allow,
Was taught to cook, learned to wash,
Kept busy around the house.
Along with our homework,
We had to study the good book,
Without common sense she reasoned,
"You can't pour piss out of a boot."
Now I am older and so is she,
Many times she made me mad,
Yet throughout life's experiences,
Grandma's foresight has made me glad.

# I WOULD

I would cherish and love you, as you never dreamed before,
I would be faithful, honest, understanding, and loyal
always.
I would share my successes, not blame you for my failures,
Support you in your endeavors, seek your support in
accomplishing mine.
I would be your best friend as well as your lover,
Seek the opportunity to be the best with one who deserves
the best.
I will ask God to enable me to do all these things;
With Him, fail you I shall not.

# IN ESSENCE

The essence of life is the essence of love.
Life cannot exist without this precious element.
It is the foundation of all existence.
God's love for humanity, man's loves for Him and
one another keeps the foundation intact.
Love cares for the unwanted, unneeded,
underprivileged and the undeserving.
Love creates, multiplies and divides.
It is the basis for hope, faith and joy in all
that we do and all that we are.

Violence and hatred spawns when there is
a lack of these basic ingredients.
Yet, evil flees from love's light.
It bonds relationships otherwise bound for destruction.
In our hearts, minds, and spirits there exists an
overwhelming desire to love and be loved,
To share and to harbor love.
It exists because we exist. Love can never die for it creates life.
Even in death, the Love of God can bring forth new life,
A new beginning and an eternal soul.

Thus, as we travel throughout this life's journey, let love roam free.
Let it grow and most of all let it guide you.
It will not lead you wrong.

# INSPIRED BY ROOTS

Everyone has a beginning; it is only fair I know mine.

I am in the present and seek the future;

however my past is locked in time.

I am of African blood, yet I bear a European name,

Along the line there has been a mistake, tell me, who is to blame?

It is said my ancestors were brought from the "Dark"

Continent to the land of the "free,"

Toiled day and night their bodies in chains, for freedom

They were not to see.

They bore children to whom the dream of freedom was passed to.

These children took this dream and made it come true!

The dream now part reality was kept that they may not soon forget,

Slavery is for those who are weak; the road to freedom is not easy yet.

Many know their history and how it came to be,

The Dream of Freedom will always live within me.

# IT IS YOU

Oh Lord, the Creator of all mankind, high and mighty,
Yet low and humble, sheds mercy upon those
of us who are wicked and mean.
How can You, Oh Lord, be so kind and just?
It is You who created the immense universe,
no one can imagine how vast.
It is You in the beginning that made life so simple, pure, and free.
It is You who made Your most astonishing creation: Human.
Yet it was humanity that succumbed to the
evil and wicked ways of Satan.
It is You who gave humanity a second chance, by sending
Your only begotten Son to die so that we may live.
Oh Lord, tell me-how can one be so Almighty, yet so forgiving?
You are so loving and almighty,
Only you can do these things
In God, in You, we surely trust.

# LADY IN MY DREAMS

I have often thought of you,
Long before I knew your name.
Visions of you appeared before my face,
As I walked in the cool of the garden lane.
Oh how I longed for your gentle touch,
And to hear the laughter of your voice,
Your playful affections and sense of humor,
Making my heart merry and rejoice.
Sometimes I think and wonder,
How all this should come to be,
As the months roll by and years pass,
Hoping that your love would find me.
Suddenly, there you were in the midst,
Appearing very real in my dream,
Silky smooth and holding me close,
Fulfilling my deepest need.
Alive I become and then I awoke,
Hoping not a moment too soon,
Only to find you had come and gone,
Into a midnight sky lit by the moon.

# EARNING A LIVING

The long days and even longer nights, suppresses
my heart's desire for freedom.
Freedom to explore, escape the chains that bind us all,
The bondage called "earning a living" while giving up our lives.
The deception that enslaves us to a place and time,
The birds fly free, the lions roar in the
jungle, deer run in the wilderness.
Yet I know we sell our freedom to the lowest
bidder. What price is freedom?
Who can pay for that which is freely given?
Stop and smell the flowers while in a rush
to our slave posts…I think not.
Day dreams rapidly descending into nightmares.
Time oh so precious being counted instead of being enjoyed.
Time wasted, so little invested.
Wisdom and folly; both competing for our imaginations,
Each of us has a limited amount of time to work with.
Relationships sacrificed on the altar of getting
ahead, attaining more and achieving less.
Shall I allow another day with new opportunities to
experience my God-given freedom to end with me being a
slave to the worldly system called…"earning a living?"

# MAMA'S CHILD

Drugs, drugs, everywhere,
Mama's child is dead.
At home, at school, people don't care,
Mama's child is dead.
Coke, crack-he did it all,
Mama's child is dead.
Pot, wine, having a ball,
Mama's child is dead.
Quit school at age ten,
Mama's child is dead.
Plenty of money, too much to spend,
Mama's child is dead.
Lookout by day, dealing at night,
Mama's child is dead.
Being in a gang made it all right,
Mama's child is dead.
Wasted his life on a deal blown,
Mama's child is dead.
Lived hard, died young,
Mama's child is dead.
Mama don't cry, Mama don't moan,
Mama's child is dead.
Mama still have six at home,
Mama's child is dead.

# MY HEART REACHES FOR THE SKY

While my feet remain grounded,
The world is spinning all around me,
Yet I am still, so very still.
Flashes of brilliance streak through my mind,
Dividing the dark recesses of the inner conscious.
Hope and Despair often seems as one,
Love and Hate are my constant companions.
I dare not dream for reality is life's master,
I am of substance; I am of spirit,
Both fighting for command of my soul.
The procession of treasure chests containing
joys, hopes and dreams, have since become
caskets of pain, despair and reality.
My soul aches, oh how it aches for peace.
Peace from within, peace from without.
Talk to my love, such a foolish notion!
Speak to me of joy, can such be found?
The rambling thoughts of a dissatisfied soul,
Blessed with the wisdom, cursed with knowledge.
Can anyone understand? Do you, Reader, understand?
Does anyone care? Do you, Reader, care?
Of course not, then again, maybe you do.

# MY SOUL

Sweet moments, quiet time,
Thoughts fleeting across my mind.
I can feel the blood rushing through my veins,
My heart pumping oxygen to my brain.
My eyes are closed, it is dark inside,
Yet a light begins to shine.
Within I search my body whole, the source of the light is my soul!
It sparkles while stars dance around,
I can hear a sweet melody sound.
As I listen, a smile creeps upon my face,
I realize my soul is full of happiness.
If you see me sad, don't feel sorry for me,
Deep inside, my soul is happy.

# STIR UP YOUR GIFT

"This is why I remind you to fan into flames the
spiritual gift God gave you..." 2 Tim. 1:6 (NLT)

A gift becomes a gift when it's given away,
Stir up the gift in you.
Every person has been gifted by our Creator,
Stir up the gift in you.
Share the gifts of love, joy, laughter and hope,
Stir up the gift in you.
For a gift to be of value a generous giver
and excellent receiver is needed,
Stir up the gift in you.
You are gifted with talents and abilities the world is sorely in need of,
Stir up the gift in you.
Exercise your gifts as a force for good,
Stir up the gift in you.
Sing your song, dance your dance, and speak your word,
Stir up the gift in you.
Write your story, play your instrument,
Stir up the gift in you.
Fight injustice, defend the oppressed, be a voice for the voiceless,
Stir up the gift in you.
Let the light shine on your gifts so others may be blessed,
Stir up the gift in you.
You are uniquely gifted for such a time as this,
Stir up the gift in you.
Allow passion be your hallmark and humility your foundation,
Stir up the gift in you.

Let not fame nor fortune be your motive for sharing,
Stir up the gift in you.
Instead let it be an act of gratefulness to the One who gifted you,
Stir up the gift in you!

# STRONG LOVE

Love is always there, the feeling never dies,
It is a strong feeling, consumes your whole life.
I know you've been brokenhearted, that's okay,
His love was not true, wouldn't have lasted anyway.
He left you weak, full of sad memories,
You are looking for the door leading to true love; take me,
I have the key.
Please give me the chance to prove how I feel,
My love for you is strong, it is so real.
You need a strong love with you day by day,
I want to be your strong love in every way.

# SUNRISE

Sunrise slowly creeping through my window pane,
It's golden beam awakening me to a new day.
Giving me hope and inspiration anew,
Providing another opportunity to see my life through.
Some take sunshine for granted but I cannot,
We are promised one day at a time that is all we got.
I enjoy each sunrise as though it were my first,
I am blessed to be alive on God's green earth.
Thus, when sunset arrives signaling another day's end,
I give thanks to God for a beautiful day again.
If I awake in the morning and the dark clouds are hiding sunrise rays,
I will thank God for waking me up to a brand new day.

# THE POET

The Poet is one who seeks to understand themselves,
Their environment and those they interact with.
A Poet has courage to express their inner
thoughts verbally and in writing.
The Poet exposes themselves to the open criticism of others. Yet,
it is the Poet who expresses what others would like to say but
cannot for whatever reasons they may have. Like the songwriter,
music can be applied to the words of a Poet. The melody must
originate from within. It is how they view life through their eyes,
feelings, thoughts, and most of all their heart. Just as one can find
strength in love, hope, and others, it too can be found in poetry.

# THE PUZZLE

Life is a puzzle…
Pieces here, pieces there.
Each representing a part of life.
Without one piece,
The puzzle is not complete.
The puzzle begins with birth, growing, learning,
hurting, crying, loving, and hating.
Added are ups, downs, knowing, not knowing, caring and not caring.
Unlike the puzzle,
Life cannot be broken down
And put together again,
For the final piece in the puzzle of life is…
Death. Or is it?

# THE RIVER

Warm and placid,
Winding like a snake.
Slowly moving,
Much time it can take.

It has seen it all,
Through the years gone by.
Generations come and pass,
They live, they die.

Sometimes it gets angry,
Consumes all in its wake.
Today it is peaceful,
Winding like a snake.

# THE WINDS OF CHANGE

Nothing is certain in life, except the certainty of change,
The people we love, those we hate, none stay the same.
We try to evolve with the foolish notion we can remain,
Our lives must constantly struggle with the winds of change.

Too often we rely on the promises of others,
Empty vases filled with lies.
We place our hope, faith, and dreams in these,
only to see them wither, fade and die.

No one, but no one can give us happiness,
though their intentions may be sane.
The most anyone can give is their very best,
For soon will come the winds of change.

The wind hurl sands of hurt into our eyes,
And bring the coldness that hardens the heart,
We shudder at the idea of being left out in the cold,
While the howling wind batter our thoughts.

We are to put on our overcoat of confidence,
And turn up the collar of love.
Place on our heads the cap of understanding,
And pray that our joy be instilled from above.

Nothing is certain in life except the certainty of change,
The storms will come and the winds shall blow,
Yet our hopes, faith and love can remain,
If anchored to The Rock during the winds of change.

# TIME

Time is the essence of life we have no control of,
It is not created by human hands, only by the good Lord above.
For children, it seems, that Ol' Man Time passes too slow
For them to achieve their goals,
To adults, the culprit passes too quickly for it means growing old.
Many have searched for that fountain of youth
that would slow Mr. Time down,
Years come, centuries pass yet that mystery has never been found.
Who do we fool? Who do we deceive? Only ourselves.

# TO MY QUEEN

From the moment my eyes gazed upon you,
I knew you were destined to be a part of me
The grace and manner in which you carried yourself,
Only served as a reminder of how I imagined you to be.

The softness of your voice and twinkle in your eyes,
Brought a pleasant smile to my face.
To behold the beauty of your silky brown skin,
Has made an impression that can never be erased.

When the soul of a man connects with the spirit of a woman,
Something supernatural takes hold.
A divine spark that originates in the heart,
Ignites a fire deep within each soul

Pretenders and fakers have approached you,
Only to discover they were no match for what is real.
I am so thankful that God preserved your integrity,
until such time I could arrive with our destiny sealed.

Your compassion for others and passion for our love,
speaks volumes about who you are.
In a few moments my life has been changed,
with renewed hope and joy instilled from God above.

In a short span of time you have filled,
the emptiness of a lonely man.
I praise my God in heaven for loving me so,
that He would present to me such a beautiful woman.

I dare not dishonor or disrespect
the gift God has given me in you,
From now until eternity
I will treasure and love unconditionally
through Christ this I shall do.

# TO YOU

Your eyes contain a sparkle which is very bright,
Your smile can bring sunshine into the night.
You are a beautiful person; I want you to know,
I adore the essence of your being; I won't ever let you go.
I am not a famous person nor do I care to be,
The only fame I seek is you loving me.
Don't consider me foolish; only a wise man cares for love.
I cherish you very much, even the angels know above.
I pray someday we shall be together,
For you will be always on my mind.
I only hope to see you again,
If it is the Lord's will, I have time.

# UNTITLED

Isn't it tragic when we have misfortunes and
someone comes to our comfort,
We forget the act of kindness?
The sun begins to shine upon us again, doesn't it?
Isn't it unfortunate that we turn our back on
those who helped us in our hour of need?
We all have commitments; so did those who gave their time willingly.
Some people have lost a great part of their lives,
Yet no one would know it by their outward expressions.
A smile does not always mean that everything is fantastic.
It's just that frowning doesn't help the matter any.
Let us not be fooled by every beaming gesture;
Deep down inside, some are crying out for help.
We should never assume if a person needs us,
They will ask.
Many times we won't let ourselves be inquired upon.
There is no need to go on assumptions.
Why not question the person?
Who knows-that the person may need you.
I do.

# WORDS

Words, words, words everywhere…a deluge of words.
What do they convey? What message do they send?
What words can I use to express what I truly feel?
Words, words so many words. The dictionary is full of them.
Yet none fully capture the essence of my innermost thoughts.

People talk, few listen and not much is being said.
Words spew from the electronic box,
Overflow on paper, always in my face.
Consonants, syllables, big words, small ones,
words with double meaning.
Words of humor and words of pain.
We encourage ourselves with words, destroy each
other with the same words… "I love you."
Build up and tear down using words.

Words running through my mind, what do I say? How do I say it?
Words of blessing, words of cursing.
We withhold words that should be said, say
words that need to be withheld.
I need not many words, just a word. A sound and meaningful word.
A word that consists of love, hope, peace, joy and faith.

A word of grace and mercy. God knew and knows
I needed a word, not just any word.
In a word, He gave me the Word.
The Word that encompasses and transcends all words… Jesus.

# LOVE IS EVERYTHING

Love shielded me in a time of danger,
Love freed me from the chains that enslaved me.
Love set my feet on solid ground,
Love forgave and restored me.
Love gave me hope in a seemingly hopeless situation,
Love prayed for and comforted me.
Love stood by when others forsake me,
Love didn't run out when trouble came in.
Love kept on giving when I needed it most,
Love believed in me at a time I didn't believe in myself.
Love humbled and in due time exalted me,
Love binded up my broken heart and healed my wounded spirit.
Love gave me life when others sought to take it away,
Love chose to bring out the best in me.
Love gave me a new beginning to live life anew,
Love smiled and showed favor upon me.
Love restored joy and peace to my aching soul,
Love reassured that my dreams still awaited me.
Love called me by name,
Love withheld no good thing from me.
Love not only makes the world go around…love created the world,
Love is my all in all for God is love.
What has love got to do with it? Everything!
Love is more than enough.

# ODE TO OPRAH

You are a precious jewel,
once a diamond in the rough.
Life has shaped and molded you
to become a source of caring and love.
You touch countless lives daily,
your genuine compassion shining through.
Giving inspiration and hope to many,
enabling dreams to come true.
God has truly blessed you with
lovely eyes and a beautiful smile,
You a woman of distinction possessing charm, class and style.
You are not an overnight sensation,
yet you were born to be a star.
You are admired the world over,
by people near and far.
This poem is simple, not for fanfare or show,
you've become a source of inspiration,
Just thought I would let you know.

Printed in the United States
by Baker & Taylor Publisher Services